A Beginner's Gui

Your Path to a Meaningful Life

Duangta Wanthong Mondi

Published by Russ Crowley

A Beginner's Guide to Buddhism

http://www.teachermondi.com

Copyright © 2015 Russ Crowley, Bangkok

Edited by Russ Crowley, Red Dragon Publishing

ISBN: 978-1-908203-17-5
ISBN: 978-1514784716 (CreateSpace-assigned ISBN)

Why You Should Read This Book

This short beginner's guide to Buddhism is written in a straightforward way to help you learn and understand about Buddhism, its history, its essence, as well as the training, and the teaching guides.

Buddhism is something that you can practice wherever you are; and, as it is based principally on teachings of compassion and wisdom, can help you towards achieving peace and meaning in your own life.

About The Author

Duangta Wanthong Mondi is Thai and a Buddhist. She grew up and lives in a rural area in North-east of Thailand, where she works as an English teacher in a Thai State school. Duangta's family are also Buddhists, and her father has been an ordained Buddhist monk for over 10 years.

For more about the author and her books, refer to page 62.

Dedicated to you.

Table of Contents

"Don't use Buddhism to become a Buddhist. Use Buddhism to become better at whatever else in your life you are doing already."

His Holiness the XIV The Dalai Lama

BUDDHA

Chapter 1.   History and Essence of Buddhism

Learning about how Buddhism began is a key step in learning and understanding more about it and its principles. Indeed, much has been written about Buddhism, but in this first chapter I give an overview of its beginnings and its key elements. This includes the history of Lord Buddha; The Threefold Training which form the backbone of the discipline, doctrine, and moral code that Lord Buddha spoke about; and, also how the principles and approach of Buddhism have not only been adapted over time, but how they both relate to, and support, modern scientific principles.

History of Lord Buddha

The history of Lord Buddha talks about his birth, his journey and practices, and then his death. These are important to know because by understanding the prince's background and upbringing, we can better comprehend the magnitude of his decision to seek an end to suffering, the trials he faced on his path, and how, by trial and error, he finally understood the fundamental truths that led to enlightenment.

Birth of Buddha

The birth of Buddha takes us back to 6th century BCE, to a small kingdom in India close to the Himalayan Mountains, which was ruled by King Sudhodhana of the Shakya clan. One night, his Queen, Mahamaya, had a dream where she saw a white elephant descend from heaven and enter her body from the side.

According to the Indian beliefs' system, an elephant symbolizes a number of extraordinary traits, including power, physical and mental strength, wisdom, sharp memory, exceptional mental capacity and learning ability and patience. However, not only does the elephant possess such remarkable qualities, but it is also aware that it does possess these features. Furthermore, its white colour, which symbolizes purity and peace, makes the appearance and actions of the elephant even more special.

As such, when Queen Mahamaya informed King Sudhodhana about her dream, he too sensed that this dream could not be dismissed as something trivial or merely ordinary. So, he summoned all the sages and holy men of his kingdom to interpret the Queen's dream.

All of the wise and holy men proclaimed that the dream was a clear indication that the Queen would become pregnant with a child who would be endowed with the elephant's exceptional traits, and who would grow up to become a symbol of purity and peace.

Shortly afterwards, Queen Mahamaya was indeed pregnant with her child; and, when she was full term—as per tradition—she knew she must travel to her parent's home to give birth. When she was en-route from Kapilavasthu, the capital city of her husband and King, to her parent's place with her entourage she passed an enchanting place called Lumbini. The sight of the blossoms bright, rich colours, the unadulterated air, the welcoming sounds of the chirping birds and the fragrance there had a magical effect on her. Queen Mahamaya felt so captivated by the sights and sounds there that she commanded her entourage to halt their journey and to spend some time there. No sooner did she step into the area, when she entered into labour and gave birth to a baby boy in the lap of nature itself (Lumbini would later become one of the holy places of Buddhism). The birth of this boy was both magical and mystical because, soon after his birth, instead of crying like most newborns, he took seven steps; in itself this is unheard of, but when he spoke, it was as if he was announcing to the world that a leader like none other was born.

His Journey from Prince to Enlightened One

King Sudhodhana named his son Siddhartha, which means "one who is capable of achieving his aim"; and, as predicted Siddhartha's birth was followed by abundance, prosperity and happiness throughout the kingdom.

A week after the birth of Siddhartha, his mother passed away and he was placed under the care of his mother's sister and step-mother, Mahaprajapati, who brought him up with utmost love and affection.

All the sages and wise men with whom King Sudhodhana consulted said wonderful things about the newborn Siddhartha. However, a great sage named 'Asita' on seeing the child, though willing to proclaim that Siddhartha would grow up to be a man of exceptional qualities, stopped short of declaring that he would grow up to be a great King: Siddharthas' stars showed that he would be greater, maybe even becoming a great saint who would, in later years, change the fate of millions.

The King loved his son and, determined to see him become his successor, kept him surrounded by unimaginable luxuries and prevented access to anything bad or unpleasant. Consequently, all Siddhartha experienced was beauty, health, wealth, happiness and luxury—in abundance. He was truly brought up in such a manner and style that he was deliberately shielded from even the sights, sounds, or smells of suffering and misery.

He was further trained in all disciplines and skills necessary to achieve kinghood: he studied under only the best teachers, he gained expertise in the arts of war, and he displayed the required intellect and power to make him a great king. Siddhartha's father, with an intention to push him further into this materialistic world, even married him to Yashodhara, a beautiful princess. It was soon all to change.

The Four Signs

One day, as Prince Siddhartha was travelling around his kingdom with his personal attendant, he encountered four things he had never seen before: an old man; a sick person; a corpse being transported in a funeral procession; and an ascetic who, despite living in the midst of so much of pain and suffering, appeared to be composed and full of peace, joy and compassion.

These 'four signs' left an indelible impression on both him and his mind—they changed him and his outlook towards life forever.

Suddenly, he came face to face with something from which he was kept away for such a long time, something he had never experienced before—suffering. From his attendant, he came to understand that suffering is indeed common in life and that death was inevitable for every single person who comes into this world.

So, at the age of 29, Siddhartha left his wife, his own newborn son, as well as the comfort and safety of his palace, and set out in search of truth and answers to his questions on human suffering

His quest for answers to his questions led him to join and study with two saintly gurus; but, he was left dissatisfied with their practices, sensing that they were leading him nowhere. He then left the two gurus and joined a group of five ascetics who were practicing austerities. While with the ascetics, Siddhartha practiced self-mortification for some time, but still remained clueless about the answers to his questions on suffering. So, with an even firmer intention to understand the truths of life, he decided to intensify his search efforts and stopped taking food and water.

One day, and struck by the pitiable condition of Siddhartha, a peasant girl put in front of him a bowl of sweet rice and pleaded with him to eat the food. It was at that moment that Siddhartha realized the futility of practicing austerities and extremes. Subsequently, he changed his mind and his mode of seeking answers and decided to keep away from, or avoid, all extremes. Siddhartha adopted the middle path when seeking his answers. He ate the bowl of rice that was offered, then bathed and changed into fresh clothes, following which he sat for meditation. After sitting in meditation for many days, truth eventually dawned on Siddhartha: all his questions regarding human suffering had been answered; and, on this full moon day, at the age of 35, Siddhartha became the enlightened one—The Buddha.

Death of Buddha

For about seven weeks following his enlightenment, Buddha spent his time in solitude. At the end of this period, the Buddha decided to deliver his first sermon to the five ascetics he had joined and then left, for they too were still practicing austerities while seeking and striving for the enlightened path.

So he travelled to Sarnath where, still at the age of 35, Lord Buddha delivered his first sermon to them. He continued to spread his message and word for the next 45 years. During these years he initiated thousands of believers into the Buddhist tradition, including his step-mother and aunt, Mahaprajapati; his wife, Yashodhara; his father, Sudhodhana; and his young son Rahula.

Despite his advancing age, the Buddha continued to travel to spread his word. The teachings he gave and the sermons he delivered were preparing for the next generation of Buddhist believers.

One of the Buddha's disciples, Ananda, was serving him and realized that Buddha was growing old. He said to Buddha that it was surprising how the Buddha's complexion was losing its brightness, how the Buddha's skin had become wrinkled, and how the Buddha's eyes, nose, ears, and tongue were also diminishing. Buddha replied that it was the law of nature and our body's must abide by those laws. Furthermore, he said that the law dictates that a young body is subject to aging, a healthy body at some point is subject to sickness, and a hale and hearty body is subject to death: these are realities and no-one is an exception to this law.

"I am old, worn out like a dilapidated cart held together with this straps."

"All things change. Whatever is born is subject to decay."

The Buddha wanted his disciples to realize that death was an inevitable part of life and that they should not lose sight of what their real purpose in life was. What's more, he asked them to see things as they are and not lose sight of the reality

Buddha became unwell at Kushinagara, a village in India that borders Nepal, and couldn't travel beyond that. He rested in a grove full of beautiful trees, laying down on the side with his head resting on his right hand and his left hand resting on his body. His last words to his disciples were:

"It may be that after I am gone that some of you will think, 'now we have no teacher.' But that is not how you should see it. Let the Dharma and the discipline that I have taught you be your teacher. All individual things pass away. Strive on, untiringly."

Lying in this posture, the Buddha breathed his last on a full moon day. This posture later came to be known as the Buddha's Nirvana.

Throughout his life, Buddha had been preparing his disciples to be their own teachers, teaching them about morals, discipline and doctrine. However, not once did he nominate anybody to serve as his successor or as a leader of the *sangha* (association or community). Once, Ananda, his most intimate devotee talked to him about choosing a person who would be able to succeed and lead after the Buddha had passed away; Buddha replied that he had taught Dharma to all alike and that there should not be any one person who could serve as authority to the remaining Buddhists. He then went on to say that that every Buddhist should try to be his own refuge instead of trying to seek that from an external agent.

> *"Make my teaching your light! Rely upon it; do not depend upon any other teaching. Make of yourself a light. Rely upon yourself, do not depend upon anyone else."*

The Threefold Training

One of the things which Buddha said while addressing his disciples during his last moments was to consider his teachings after he is gone, and to hold on to them steadfastly; in particular, he emphasised discipline and doctrine.

Discipline according to the Buddhist philosophy, and as described by Buddha himself, is the moral/ethical code of conduct that moulds our speech and our actions—this is what Buddhists refer to as sila, or *moral training*. Equally, Buddha also placed emphasis on doctrine—the development of man's ability to tame and control his mind. To achieve control over the mind, the doctrine comprises two components:

- cultivating concentration (*Samadhi*)

- developing wisdom (*Panna*).

This cultivation of concentration and developing wisdom are what are called *training in higher mentality* and *training in higher wisdom* respectively.

Various manifestations, or indications, of a troubled mind include jealousy, hatred, greed, ego, and ignorance. However, these manifestations can be eliminated by cultivating, developing, and perfecting our ethics, mentality and wisdom by *training in higher morality, training in higher concentration,* and *training in higher wisdom,* respectively. When adopted and carefully followed they can lead the mind to a desired tranquil state. Together, these are known as **threefold training** (or Trisikkha) and, as they are interdependent, cannot function without crossing each other's paths.

These are the principles which Buddha urges his disciples to never abandon because, when followed carefully, these ensure the passage of man to a higher level in his life (and is why the word 'higher' is attached to each of them).

These three go hand in hand because it is only when a person can straighten his ethics/morality that he will he be able to strengthen his concentration; and, it is only when he has mastered his meditation that his hunger for wisdom will be satisfied.

Training in Higher Morality

Though love and compassion serve as a foundation for *sila* (morality/moral training), it's not just about loving and having compassion for one's near and dear. No, it is only when one can make no distinction in passing their love and compassion to others not related to them, will there be a success of morality. Moreover, only when one loves everybody as if they were his own will they not think of doing anything that can either hurt, or cause pain and suffering

Training in moral conduct or morality involves 3 essential elements: *right speech, right action,* and *right livelihood.*

Right Speech

Right speech deals with using the right words, the right language, communicating appropriately, always speaking the truth, being fearless about speaking the truth, and being fearless about accepting and embracing the truth.

Naturally, to be able to speak, face and accept the truth requires an element of will power and mental strength to face the backlash. Yet, possessing the will to adhere to what is right will engender the needed strength to go on to lead an ethical and moral life.

Right speech also refers to abstaining from talking ill of others to either spoil their reputation, tarnish their image, assassinate their character, develop hatred, or create a rift between people. Let's be clear, right speech means not disturbing the harmony and tranquillity of somebody's mind with one's own talk; it is about avoiding making the minds of others restless and agitated (as evidenced when seeking revenge). Furthermore, right speech is also about refraining from speaking ill of others without any basis, of jealousy, and to do so with the sole intention of creating a negative perception of them in the view of others.

Right speech is about not engaging in a rude, rash, and impolite talk or discussion that could hurt the feelings of others.

Right speech is about speaking after a lot of thinking, contemplation, and consideration. Right speech is never about using profane language that could in any way disturb the mind of the person using it and at whom it is targeted.

Right speech is about adopting language and tone that is genuinely pleasant, friendly, filled with warmth, love, affection, concern, compassion, that is sensible, and is unpretentious.

Right speech requires one to speak only when required and to utter only what is essential and where it is necessary. Finally, right speech implies that if one does not have anything worthy of saying or the time is inopportune then the noblest thing to do would be to maintain silence.

Of course, before one can determine the right speech in any given situation, it is important to first appreciate and understand the right action.

Right Action

Right action is about knowing and choosing the correct decision in any given situation. What's more, it's about taking the correct decisions with integrity, and choosing what is right irrespective of how hard and difficult the path is to traverse. It is also about having and maintaining a firm conviction to both make the right decision and to achieve that action without wavering.

In addition, right action also refers to selecting and heading off on the honourable path no matter how difficult it actually is or how many hardships you are forced to face. It is also concerned with not engaging in actions that could disrupt the lives of others, be they humans or animals (whether hunting or not), and cheating people.

Simply put, if pleasure can only be derived at the cost of others then it is not the right action.

Right Livelihood

Right livelihood deals with confining oneself only to those activities and professions which are legal and do good to humanity. Similarly, right livelihood refers to avoiding activities which could cause suffering or endanger people, animals, or the environment, including rejecting professions or activities that are illegal, such as human trafficking, kidnapping, murder, or dealing in drugs and substances

Additionally, right livelihood is about refraining from making a living by doing business and things that could prove harmful to others. These include: dealing in arms, weapons, ammunition, making destructive material, dealing in drugs and alcohol, human trafficking, engaging underage children in work, robbery, thefts, murder and kidnapping.

To summarise *Training in Higher Morality,* Buddha teaches us that practicing virtue in our speech, in conducting ourselves in the way we approach and do things, and in living correctly enables us to live both morally and ethically; and, without these our journey for a meaningful life, and ultimate spirituality will end even before it has begun.

Buddha always said that it is better to die rather than to break our ethics and morals because death brings an end to just one life, but breaking our morals will affect our karma and could set us back several lives and destroy our opportunity to experience happiness in this life and in many lives to come.

Training in Higher Mentality

As was mentioned, morality can be strengthened by reigning in our speech, our actions, and the way we lead our daily lives; unfortunately, though these are indeed steps in the right direction, more is required.

You see, it's quite possible that a person may not say anything wrong or bad, and they may not do anything that is offensive, obnoxious, or bad, but that doesn't mean the person is pure in their thoughts; and, this is where training in mentality comes into play. If a person's speech sounds enchanting, and their visual display is appealing, it may mask what is beneath the surface—their inner thoughts oppose their outward display. However, if their thoughts are aligned with their pure persona, then naturally the outcome will be purity in mind, as well as speech and actions. Likewise, if the source itself is bad then the outcome can be corrupt or contaminated; so, it is essential to be trained in focussing our mental state/concentration.

Training in mentality refers to not only developing the right thoughts, but also keeping the right thoughts alive all the time, as well as keeping the negative thoughts at bay. To be precise, the three components that comprise training in higher mentality are: *right effort*, *right mindfulness*, and *right concentration*.

Right Effort

Right effort is required to keep the bad, unsavoury, or unhealthy thoughts under control. It is important to instil effort and exert oneself to prevent the above thoughts entering the mind. As we all know, bad thoughts do crop up, so right effort also involves nipping them in the bud when they do arise, as well as improving one's own store of good thoughts: putting a determined effort in maximising the store of good thoughts and minimising the store of bad ones is both a helpful and good practice.

Right Mindfulness

Being constantly on the guard to watch for any disturbing, distracting thoughts trying to find a place in the mind. Right mindfulness plays a prominent role in furthering one's spiritual progress.

Right mindfulness and Right effort together lead to the next essential component in Mentality which is Right concentration

Right Concentration

The purpose of concentration is to remain unperturbed, unfazed, and unbothered in all scenarios, circumstances, and conditions. Your focus needs to be on spiritual enhancement and progress and to try not to let anything come in their way. As you may realise, it's common for people who are experiencing suffering to be spiritually inclined and to develop indifference for everything; yet, when the situation is good they quickly reengage with their materialistic pursuits again putting their spiritual journey and well-being firmly behind them. However, when one is focused on a spiritual path then both good and bad times alike are treated equally and the person appears indifferent to the circumstances.

To summarise, regardless of circumstances, a focused person is happy, joyous, peaceful, calm and composed.

Training in Higher Wisdom

No matter how much a person has read, how good their learning capacity is, how intelligent they are, how good they are at talking, how sweet their words are, how much knowledge they have acquired, how much others look up to them for their erudition and learning, they are not a person of wisdom if they are bothered by disturbing, disrupting and distracting thoughts. Only a person who has reigned in their thoughts (a situation where a person controls their thoughts and their thoughts do not control them) is a person of wisdom. Buddha said that only a fool will consider them-self most intelligent and learned and yet fall prey to their own disrupting thoughts.

Right Understanding

True wisdom is about being able to differentiate and understand what is real, what gives real happiness, and what provides permanent joy. It is also about developing an insight into the simple truths of life and conducting oneself accordingly.

Right Thoughts

Correct thoughts that do not stem from negative feelings and emotions, such as jealousy, hatred and anger, form the basis for wisdom. Ultimately, a person's essential aim should be their spiritual progress and enlightenment, and whatever is either not helping or hindering them in their spiritual pursuit should be filtered and thrown out.

People can be learned and intelligent but if they are not using that intelligence wisely, perhaps only to eat and sleep well, to settle scores with their enemies, to make more enemies, etc., then having those attributes is of little use.

To close this training section, wisdom is the one faculty that differentiates us from animals, but if it either remains unused or is used incorrectly, then it is simply wasted. It should be used to expedite kindness to all, to generate and spread love and compassion, and to discover how to end suffering, both for oneself and for others.

The Principles of Buddhism and Principles of Science

> *"Buddhism is not a collection of views. It is a practice to help us eliminate wrong views."*

Thich Nhat Hanh, The Heart of Buddha's Teaching

As I will show shortly, there are a number of similarities between the principles of Buddhism and the principles of Science, but a key element to appreciate is that Buddhism is very adaptive. Indeed, as the Dalai Lama said, *"If scientific analysis were conclusively to demonstrate certain claims in Buddhism to be false, then we must accept the findings of science and abandon those claims."* (Lama, 2006). As such, as the world evolves, and new findings are unearthed, then Buddhism must also adapt to this new knowledge. The following shows 10 areas where similarities exist:

1. **Impossible to Fail:** Science requires insight, reasoning, and effort (or perseverance). As you may already realise, there is no place for failure in science, because not finding success in an experiment or investigation cannot be termed failure it's just proof that this particular process does not

work in favour of the experiment. So, without getting disheartened and armed with new hope, new vigour, new methodologies, and new hypotheses, scientists move on to testing for success in what they are trying to do, be it trying to invent something, discover, or prove.

Similarly, Siddhartha did not know what the results would be when he first started his journey on the spiritual path; but, he persisted. In the same way as scientists explore, he was curious, inquisitive, thirsty for knowledge, and hungry for finding the solutions to his questions. However, he was not worried about the time frame, and he was not concerned about getting quick results, rather seeking an everlasting solution. During his quest, he did not hesitate to experiment and 'fail'; but, more importantly, his determination was intact, and he did not quit. With each 'setback', he modified his methodology and finally, after 6 long years, he attained enlightenment – he proved his theory.

2. **Inner Potential:** As the science fraternity believes, science holds key to endless discoveries, inventions, innovations and possibilities. What is required to unlock these advancements is an analytical bent of mind, an investigative nature, and perseverance. Accordingly, they believe and support their inner strength rather than reliance on any external agent.

Buddha too believed that there is an immense potential lying latent in every person, and all that is required to tap that intrinsic potential is not divine intervention, but the belief in oneself.

3. **Verification:** One of the foundations of science is verification, the ability to repeat and confirm results. To be able to verify results, science needs data, research, hypothesis, experimentation, and evidence—it requires proof; and, without this nothing can be interpreted or deduced. Every individual experiment is unique, which gives rise to unique experiences for the people involved in it; and, due to the differing perspectives of individuals, scientists must record their results based on their observations and not on the observations of others.

Buddha also asked his disciples not to take him as a final authority. He taught them to believe and to follow something only after they have themselves tested and verified it. He asked them to pay attention to their experiences rather than to what others have experienced or said. He said:

"Do not accept things just because I your teacher have said so. Be your own teacher."

"Monks and scholars should well analyse my words, like gold to be tested through melting, cutting and polishing. Only then should they adopt them, but not for the sake of showing me respect."

Buddhism encourages its believers (or those interested in Buddhism) to see for themselves, to test for themselves rather than relying on the observations of others. Furthermore, relying on one's own experiences enables you to absorb and follow something (principles and doctrines) because you yourself believe in it. As you yourself have tested it, you therefore find it readily acceptable...much in the same way as science talks about reasoning, gaining insight, hypotheses, testing, experimenting and validating

"Do not go upon what has been acquired by repeated hearing; nor upon tradition; nor upon rumor; nor upon what is in a scripture; nor upon surmise; nor upon an axiom; nor upon specious reasoning; nor upon a bias towards a notion that has not been pondered over; nor upon another's seeming ability; nor upon the consideration, 'The monk is our teacher.' Rather, when you yourselves know that these things are good; these things are not blamable; undertaken and observed, these things lead to benefit and happiness, then and only then enter into and abide in them."

4.   **The Universe:** Science has proven that there is a universe that is made up of planets, stars, galaxies and more.

According to Buddhism, there exists not just one world with one sun, one moon and one earth, but there are thousands of suns, moons and earths that are present in a thousand worlds.

5.   **Cause and Effect:** Both Science and Buddhism believe in the law of causality, i.e., the principle of cause and effect: something causes an event to occur, and this triggers something else to happen.

6. **No place for Superstition:** In Science there is no place for superstitious beliefs. Anything that cannot be proved, and for which evidence cannot be provided, is unfounded.

   Buddha also did away with superstitious beliefs, rituals and customs that either made no sense, which he could not relate to, or which he thought were mere adornment and cannot assist in the attainment of liberation and enlightenment.

7. **Flexibility:** Neither Science nor Buddhism are rigid, nor both have a very flexible approach. Even if a new finding disapproves of or contradicts an earlier experiment, methodology, result or conclusion, it is still accepted.

   It is much the same with Buddhism. If something contradictory to a common or accepted belief is proved then Buddhism does not hesitate to test that new idea or study, in order to understand and accept it. Anything that has been scientifically proven is acceptable in Buddhism; and, as was mentioned earlier, Buddhism must adapt itself to new theories.

   For example, centuries ago, when the common agreement was that the earth was flat and the sun revolved around the earth, Buddhists believed also; yet, when Science proved these false, Buddhists did not hesitate to change their belief.

8. **Impermanence:** Science believes in impermanence. We are all aware that change is perpetual: nature is evolving, the seasons are changing, the universe is expanding, and ultimately, on a human level, we change too—nothing is ever static, everything is in motion.

Buddhism also believes in this concept, that everybody and everything is bound to change: a child will grow into an adult, and an adult will grow old; a person who is born will not live forever; a healthy person will not retain his health forever, and so forth. Nothing is permanent, and everything will change.

9. **The Principle of Mass**: In Science, one definition of mass is the property of a physical body which determines its strength of mutual gravitational attraction on other bodies: the greater the mass of the body, the more it gets attracted to other bodies; and, as part of this process it loses some of its own energy. Also, as energy can be exchanged between particles, those with a lesser mass can draw energy more quickly.

In the same manner as Science talks about mass (and the way it is intertwined with energy), Buddhism talks about ignorance. Ignorance is something which misleads us into thinking that happiness is derived from materials, people and other transient or impermanent things...the more ignorance (or things) we have and cling onto, the greater are our suffering if they are lost; moreover, this also decrease our own chances of salvation or enlightenment.

Where Science talks about energy, Buddhism talks about happiness: we gain energy when we are happy (we attract) and we lose energy when we are sad (we repel). So, when a person is happy they attract and draw energy much quicker than when they are sad (have you noticed how happy people attract similar?) Of course, if we minimise or remove the chances or causes of our sadness, then we will naturally absorb more happiness/energy.

21

10. **Attraction:** An electric field creates a magnetic field, and vice versa (electromagnetism). In the same way these fields affect the objects around them, by either attracting or pushing them away, Buddhist principles say that our surroundings cause happiness and when happy the value of the surroundings also increases. As mentioned above, happy people attract similar, and sad people are often lonely. However, it must be said, that there is no one single source of happiness, rather there are multiple 'fields'; and, in the same way as electromagnetic fields affect different objects in different ways, different sources of happiness have different levels of attraction.

Another by-product of electric and magnetic fields is light. In this particular combination, a wave can be produced carries energy in the form of light that is radiated out.

As I'm sure you have experienced, kindness and compassion can also be radiated, producing happiness around you, as well as generating greater kindness and compassion, much in the way of a light -wave of spiritual energy.

Now we have looked at the Principles of Buddhism and Science, and seen how they align, let's quickly look at the Buddhist beliefs.

Buddhist Beliefs

There are a number of Buddhist beliefs, but here the 5 main ones:

1. Buddha is not a God.

   This is key to understanding Buddhism. Buddha neither is, nor was a God. Also, neither was he a messenger of God nor a prophet. Buddha was born an ordinary human being who set out on a path to perfect himself. He strived hard to develop kindness, compassion and peace in his believers; and, he taught and showed us that it is not impossible to overcome suffering in our lives.

Worship to Buddha is not formal. If Buddhists fold their hands or bow in front of a Buddha's statue, it is to express their gratitude and respect to him for his teachings. When they use flowers, it is to remind themselves that nothing in this world is permanent and, like flowers, everything will wilt. If they use a lamp, or candles, then this helps to remind themselves about the power of truth and knowledge.

2.   We have a purpose in life.

Buddhists believe that they are all driven by a common purpose, to end suffering in their lives.

3.   There is an afterlife that depends on the present life.

All our actions, be they good or bad, have consequences—karma. Our good actions will create a good store of merits—good karma—and our bad actions will create a bad store of merits—bad karma. Furthermore, until one attains enlightenment, life continues through rebirth and the consequences of our actions in the present life can be felt and seen in our next life. Every Buddhist should strive to end his cycle of rebirth—enlightenment or nirvana.

4.   Meditation is essential to stay connected with your mind.

There are many benefits that are associated with meditating regularly. Meditation gives us the opportunity to look deep into ourselves, which enables us to cleanse our mind, to straighten our speech, to ponder right actions and right thoughts, as well as improving our ability to focus and concentrate.

5. Staying associated with the spiritual community is important.

The spiritual community serves as a guiding force and a source of motivation; and is a place where like-minded people with similar objectives come together. The positive energy created in such places is so potent that it creates a much greater impact than reading scriptures and books alone.

๑ ร้านรักษาร้อยสิบให้
รีย์ยุขรร ๑๗๑ รันโกรัง

Chapter 2.   Buddhist Teaching Guides

The Triple Gems of Buddhism

The triple gems of Buddhism are also called as the three jewels, three treasures, three refuges, precious triad, or *Triratna* in Sanskrit.

When a person decides to become a Buddhist, the first thing they will do is to seek refuge in the three gems: Buddha, Dharma, and Sangha. They do this by stating:

I take refuge in Buddha

I take refuge in Dharma

I take refuge in Sangha.

To proclaim devotion to the three gems is to be a Buddhist. It may help to think of this like a process where a person is first initiated into Buddhism, and is where they subsequently go to get to know and to understand the historical Buddha: the Triple Gems (Buddha, Dharma, and Sangha) show the way to end suffering.

When a Buddhist believer is at this early initiation stage, they are bound more by inquisitiveness and an inquiring mode. However, it is an important step, as it is only after the person understands who Buddha is, and what the three gems actually are— how one can seek refuge, how the three gems can save a person from the misery and suffering prevalent all around—do they choose, or make the decision, to become a Buddhist. Again, it may help to think of this like an initiation into the order.

The three gems are the ideals that form the **heart of Buddhism**; and they are the principles that seek to satisfy the inquisitiveness of those who come to understand Buddha and how they can be saved from misery and suffering.

Buddha

Buddha here doesn't merely signify the founder of Buddhism/ historical Buddha. Here Buddha signifies both the enlightened Buddha as well as the centrality revolving around the idea of Buddha.

Buddha is considered to be the epitome of wisdom and a truly enlightened person. So, when a Buddhist professes to take refuge in Buddha, they mean that there is nothing better than to be enlightened and that there is nothing safer than seeking refuge in the most enlightened person. It's tantamount to taking an oath that *"I seek refuge in enlightenment to ensure my safety and security."* Indeed, going to Buddha to seek refuge is like going to the ultimate teacher to seek answers to all our questions...and is the very first step on the path to enlightenment.

The second step is the Dharma.

Dharma

Dharma, meaning 'truth' in Sanskrit, is the second gem (or the second jewel) of Triratna. Dharma is symbolized by the wheel.

The *Dharma* contains the teachings of Buddha. These teachings are based on the four *Noble Truths* which create a strong foundation for Buddhism.

The *Dharma* also emphasizes that a person is sure to be freed from the clutches of ignorance only when the 4 noble truths (that are mentioned in the Dharma) are practiced regularly. Only then can the person seek refuge in the Dharma (seeking refuge is like saying that I am safe and secure now that I have taken this refuge). As you can see, the Dharma can only protect you if your path to the truth is begun with a serious and definite intention: seeking refuge in the Dharma is seeking guidance from Buddha through his teachings, and agreeing to follow them is with a firm conviction that you will tread this path to become enlightened.

In conclusion, Dharma is about cleansing, purifying and conditioning one's mind, instilling compassion, kindness, love and ethical values.

Sangha

The *Sangha* refers to the community of monks (bhikkhus), nuns (bhikkhunis), and lay followers (male and female) who are practicing the Dharma.

The sangha shoulders the responsibility of spreading the message of Buddha out of compassion for mankind, and is guided by a strong intent to put those who believe in Buddhism on the path to enlightenment. Sangha can also include teachers who are ahead of us on the path to enlightenment and are willing to be the guiding lights that will dispel the surrounding darkness on our quest for truth. As we all know, it is helpful to have teachers to guide us and to help us as we traverse the path of dharma.

The sangha is meant to convey to others that the path of the Dharma—the path to attain enlightenment—can indeed be treaded and progress can always be made to achieve enlightenment.

The Foundational Doctrines of Buddhism

After attaining enlightenment, Buddha gave his first sermon in deer park in a place called Sarnath. This first sermon was on the four Noble Truths, which not only form the basis of Buddhism, but also hold the essence of the teachings of the Buddha

The four noble truths are as follows:

1. The truth of suffering

2. The truth of the cause of suffering

3. The truth of freedom from suffering

4. The truth of the path that leads to cessation of (freedom from) suffering

The Buddha's exposition on the four noble truths mainly focusses on ways to alleviate and to finally end the suffering which he had witnessed and experienced. His quest for an answer to the question of suffering began with him first identifying that suffering is common in life and prevalent across all cultures, regardless of wealth, health, status, or age.

The Truth of Suffering

The first truth says that suffering is present all the time and is conspicuous.

Suffering pervades through every stage of life, be it birth, death, adulthood, or old age, and it can manifest in both physical and mental forms.

Physical Suffering

Physical suffering can be caused by disease, pain, injury, sickness or age-related problems. One may be hale and hearty, but as everything is impermanent, this is only for a brief period of time. As we know, the only thing constant in this life is change: a young person will grow old, a person with youthful looks will one day lose all their charm, a healthy person will eventually lose that good health and vigour, it is a matter of time. Consequently, as the Buddha says, a person cannot be thoroughly happy even if they are enjoying good health, good looks, and in their youth, because the fear of losing these one day causes suffering.

Mental suffering

As we all know, suffering does not manifest itself in the physical form alone, it can also affect us mentally in many ways, including: sadness, depression, feelings of rejection and dejection, anger, stress, jealousy, hatred, loneliness and hopelessness. All these example are mental manifestations of suffering. It is a fact of life that we experience different levels of sadness, depending on our individual relationships and circumstances; for example, being sad about the death of a loved one, angry with someone close to us, becoming dejected about not getting what we want and desire, or even resenting or being jealous about someone achieving something we wanted ourselves—all these are mental suffering.

When Buddha spoke about suffering he did not deny that happiness is also part of life. Happiness arising out of relationships, friendships, progress in life, achievements in life, the love and respect one gets in life, and so on are all good examples; but, they too are impermanent. When happiness is gone, it again leads to sadness and suffering.

Of course, each of us is happy to be with those we love, but when it's time for them to leave, our happiness is lost leaving both an emptiness and a desperate desire for more time with your loved one—you suffer.

For material objects, such as a car. You are happy you bought the car, you feel a sense of pride in what you have, but if the car gets damaged in an accident, again you suffer.

So, the Buddha's first noble truth asks the people to identify and accept that nobody is devoid of suffering, it is common to us all, and is an integral part of life.

The Truth of the Cause of Suffering

Buddha's second noble truth says that suffering is primarily caused by ignorance and desire. They are the root causes of suffering and misery in everyone's life.

The desire for materialistic pleasures, power, fame, comforts, a healthy life without death, a life without worries, a life of abundance, desire to be above all and above everything are just few of the many yearnings we have. Unfortunately, the cycle is never-ending and the end of one desire frequently leads to the birth of another desire, and on-and-on—there are no ends to our desires. In fact, these desires, these cravings for more and more, can lead to so much of unhappiness, and discontent in our lives, that it triggers negative feelings, emotions and reactions, and agitates and robs the mind of its peace, thereby causing suffering. Again, none of the things we long for provide lasting happiness

For example, a beautiful person might desire to remain beautiful forever because being beautiful makes her very happy; but it will not last—it cannot last—because nothing is permanent. So their fading beauty causes them suffering. Sure, you can use technology to try and maintain your body and youthful look, you can go under the knife to make sure you remain beautiful, but at what price? There is the knowledge that this may be just one in a series of procedures, each more risky than the last—suffering; there may be side effects to this—suffering. So attempting to associate happiness with temporary pleasures will never ensure lasting happiness.

Ignorance, is another root cause of suffering: our inability to see reality, inability to gain insight of the reality, inability to accept the hard truths of life, inability to let the things pass as per their nature, ignorance in trying to understand the impermanent nature of life, and inability to understand the true nature of things, all leads to the same thing.

Ignorance sows seeds for desire to flourish

When the mind is controlled by desire and ignorance, it becomes so clouded that it loses the ability to think, reason and rationalise thereby triggering negative feelings, emotions, reactions, behaviours, thoughts, such as envy, jealousy, hatred, greed, avarice, or worse.

The Truth of Freedom from Suffering

The 3rd noble truth emphasizes that suffering does not have to be prevalent in one's life; it emphasises that it is possible to end that suffering.

Buddha said that suffering could be ended by getting rid of desire and ignorance. Doing so gives way to compassion and where there is compassion, there is peace and joy all around. Moreover, a person who is compassionate will not hesitate to help others seek liberation from suffering. The reality to this is that when ignorance dies, one become a person of wisdom and deep insight. Such a person sees things as they truly are and will not be affected by changes in personal circumstances, treating what would be considered both happy and sad circumstances alike.

The Truth of the Path that Leads to Cessation of Suffering

The fourth noble truth talks about the methods that should be adopted to ensure an ending to suffering in our lives. This method is called the noble **eightfold path**. The Buddha laid down eight steps for a person to practice, so that he could bring his sufferings and misery to an end and proceed on the path to enlightenment.

The Eightfold path?

We have two extremes at the opposite ends of the scale: one is over-indulgence in materialistic comforts and pleasures, which undoubtedly leads to greater desires; the other is practicing asceticism and self-mortification in the name of giving up everything. Unfortunately, both extremes actually involve more suffering and pain and are actually futile in removing suffering. Because of this, Buddha proposed that we should adopt the *middle path*; he called it the eightfold path. This eightfold path aims at developing morality, mentality and wisdom; and, as it is more effective when put to use in every aspect of life, should be practiced daily.

Doing so, is a simple yet powerful approach and will have a deep impact on a person with respect to their approach towards life. The eightfold path is as follows:

1. Right understanding
2. Right thought
3. Right speech
4. Right action
5. Right livelihood
6. Right effort
7. Right mindfulness
8. Right concentration

Following these simple yet powerful steps ensures peace, calm, knowledge, insight, enlightenment and, finally, nirvana.

We have already discussed of these before, and as we know the 2 steps of **right understanding**, and **right thought**, make up the components of good wisdom.

Developing wisdom is about encouraging the right thoughts and fostering deeper insight and understanding to help us differentiate between right and wrong, good and bad, and what should be avoided and welcomed. Wisdom is about developing a firm conviction to remain fixed on the path of truth and to see things as they really are.

Right Understanding involves going above superficial understanding and gaining deep insight. Everyone is aware that suffering is common in life, but rarely does anyone really bother to understand the causes of that suffering, and even fewer seek how they could actually put an end to their suffering. Right understanding is about understanding the real truths of life—one's purpose in life, almost. As you can see, here, we're talking about going beyond the books, scriptures and texts to obtain a deeper understanding of the true essence of life.

Right thought directs that our speech, action and decision-making should be directed by the way that we think. There is no synchronization if our thoughts say one thing and our speech/actions says another. As we have all probably experienced, speech and actions can both sound and appear virtuous, but if they originate from an unvirtuous thought, then that speech or those actions cannot be associated with wisdom. It is only if the speech or action stems from a right thought will it be genuine and pure.

The 3 steps of **right speech**, **right action**, and **right livelihood** make up the components of good conduct/morality.

To reiterate, wrong speech gives rise to lies, deceit, ill-feelings, hatred, anger, stress, tension, rift between people/groups, assassination of somebody's character and reputation. But right speech creates harmony, happiness, compassion, kindness and cordial atmosphere.

Wrong actions will harm people, society, or the environment, so should be avoided. Whereas right actions are helpful to everyone and everything.

Similarly, the wrong livelihood will cause harm and suffering to those around us; and this includes butchering, gambling, human trafficking, trading in weapons, drugs, etc. On the other hand, choosing to earn a living in a peaceful, acceptable, and productive way that can benefit you as well as the society is the desired choice. Surely the welfare and progress of all should be paramount in our choice of preferred livelihood?

The 3 steps of **right effort**, **right mindfulness**, and **right concentration** make up the components of good mentality.

Right effort involves:

- Preventing evil, disturbing and distracting thoughts from arising in the mind.

- Cleansing the mind of the existing unwanted thoughts.

- Causing good, healthy and productive thoughts to arise in the mind.

- Improving the presence of already prevalent wholesome thoughts in the mind.

Right mindfulness is about being alert and attentive to the thoughts that come and go out of the mind, being totally aware of the feelings and emotions associated with the thoughts.

Right concentration is about being focused on attaining the ultimate goal.

To summarise, the eightfold path is a systematic and stepped approach to ridding oneself of suffering and progressing one's own path to achieving enlightenment.

The Five Precepts for Living

Buddhism discourages its followers from using any action, speech or behaviour that could prove harmful to oneself, to others, or to society. The Buddhist tradition has also been built in such a manner that it encourages a person to develop a skilled mind. Doing so ensures that the person is equipped to decide or act in a manner that will not be regretful.

The five precepts for living are no different, and they leave ample scope for a person to put their skilled mind to use.

The five precepts are not rules, regulations, or commandments which, if broken, would entail punishment in a severe form. Rather, they are basic training principles, or rules, which help those preparing to become Buddhists to develop a skilled mind. Since Buddhism lays so much emphasis on the mind, the breaking of any of the rules should also be governed by the mind. It is essential that those who wish to tread the path to enlightenment have a mind that is free of guilt, regret and remorse; thereby, any decisions or actions they subsequently take will leave that person guilt free. If there is a breach, the mind should be aware of it so that remedial actions can be taken and the action would not again be repeated.

Being a flexible tradition, the Buddhist order acknowledges that several views, or angles, may be necessary to approach or understand any given situation, behaviour, or problem. Accordingly, Buddhism does not impose rigid and strict rules with respect to any course of action which one is supposed to take in a particular situation. So, instead of listing the right and wrong actions, or those that are forbidden in the Buddhist tradition, the tradition has laid out certain principles.

Since these principles are concerned with ethics, it is important to use a logical amount of sensitivity when such situations are encountered:

1. To abstain from taking the life of a living being.

    This is the most important ethical principle in Buddhism as every living being has a right to live; and Buddhism tells its followers to respect that right. Based on compassion, kindness and love, this precept discourages a Buddhist from being violent.

2. To abstain from taking what is not given or stealing.

    Stealing is one way to cause harm to others, and by stealing you are depriving a person of what is rightfully theirs. The underlying basis of this precept is generosity.

3. To abstain from sexual misconduct.

    Legal and emotional issues aside, sexual misconduct can have serious implications that include causing harm to oneself or to others, causing damage to one's reputation, breaking or misusing the commitment made to a person, and many more consequences. So this precept indicates that not only should one abstain from committing such mistake but also to discourage others from doing so to. The underlying basis of this precept is propriety.

Misconduct in this sense, can also mean abstaining from any sensual pleasure such as overeating.

4. To abstain from using harsh speech and telling lies.

Speech plays a very important role in our lives and, as such, should be used to speak the truth, and to produce gentle, encouraging and comforting words. But, sadly, speech is too often misused. This precept prevents people from lying and hurting others and is based on truthfulness.

5. To abstain from intoxicants or harmful substances.

Intoxicating drinks and drugs cloud the mind of the person consuming them. They can also diminish the judgement-taking capacity of the person and, when the person's mind is blurry, they cannot be alert and attentive.

Intoxicants can blur our judgement which can also impact the other four precepts because, in an intoxicated or inebriated condition, a person can lose control and break the training rules.

The Three Baskets of Buddha's Teachings

The word of Buddha consists of 3 aspects: doctrine, practice, and realization. It is the doctrine that makes the three baskets of Buddha's teachings. These three baskets contain Buddha's teachings, sermons, and discourses, starting with the first sermon (delivered in the deer park at Sarnath after his enlightenment) till his death, 45 years later.

The three baskets are called Tripitaka in Sanskrit. They form the basic scriptures which capture the essence of Buddhism:

- **Vinaya** – talks about the appropriate ways to behave.

- **Sutta** – what kind of thoughts to embrace and what kind of thoughts to abandon.

- **Abhidhamma** – touches upon the important and higher aspects of Buddhism and its teachings.

Origins

These teachings were written down almost 500 years after Buddha's death. Prior to that, the teachings were memorized and taught orally. When the teachings were first written down, it was onto long narrow leaves which were then sewn together and tied into bunches; these were then placed into separate baskets—hence the name 'three baskets'.

The three baskets also signify the passing down of the baskets from one generation to another generation of believers, from teacher to a believer. Each basket plays a unique role in the Buddhist tradition.

The Discipline Basket

The **discipline basket** (*Vinaya Pitaka*) because it lays down rules and regulations intended for monks and nuns at the sangha (the community of monks and nuns).

The rules and regulations laid out for the monks and nuns include details about the permitted level and form of interaction between monks and nuns, how to dress, as well as details pertaining to robe-making and other basic but essential information to help them lead a productive life at the sangha.

As was mentioned in the section about the Principles of Buddhism and Science, Buddhism is flexible and Vinaya Pitaka talks about how breaking a rule under certain conditions is not considered breach of conduct. For example, though monks are not supposed to partake of any food after noon, if they are unwell and have to eat something after midday to aid their recovery, then the rule is not considered broken.

The Discourse Basket

As the name suggests, the **discourse basket** (*Sutta Pitaka*) and, as the name itself suggests, is a collection of the discourses and sermons of Buddha, as well as transcripts of discussion and conversation which Buddha had with the monks and nuns of the Buddhist tradition. This basket aims at improving a person's thought processes, thereby helping him both welcome good thoughts and abandon disturbing thoughts.

Sutta Pitaka also has a collection of stories of past births and lives of Buddha known as Jatakas. Finally, also included in this basket is one of the most important texts, the *Dhammapada*, (Buddha's exposition on law), which comprises 423 verses containing important instructions to Buddhist believers.

Life Lessons

The life lessons (*Abhidhamma Pitaka*) are a collection of texts that clarify on subjects concerning time, matter, and mind. Altogether, the scriptures have great significance in the Buddhist tradition because they provide valuable information about how to lead one's life.

Chapter 3.   Sacred Activities

In this section we will look at the Buddhist holy days, festivals, and ceremonies.

Buddhist Holy Days

There are 4 main Buddhist holy days in a calendar year: Magha Puja, Visakha Puja, Atthame Puja, and Asalha Puja. We will look at each in turn, as well as other holy days.

Magha Puja

During the time of the Buddha, 1250 of his disciples, those who had followed in his footsteps to attain enlightenment, all came to him to pay their respects. This particular day was the first full moon day of Magha and, for this very reason, this day is observed on the first full day of every Magha (March), the 3rd lunar month in the Indian calendar.

The day is also called Sangha day in order to remember the 1250 monks who belonged to the monastic sangha. Another name you may hear Magha Puja being referred to is the 'Fourfold Assembly Day', for the following reasons:

1. All the 1250 monks were arahants (this means they were enlightened ones all of whom attained Nirvana)

2. All of them were initiated into the Buddhist tradition by Buddha himself.

3. The coming together of all the 1250 monks was unplanned and simply a matter of coincidence.

4. This event took place on the first full moon day of Magha.

Buddha delivered a sermon to the 1250 monks gathered there, and talked about good and bad actions as well as about ways to keep the mind purified. Lay-people commemorate this day by visiting temples and circumnavigating the chapel or a statue of Buddha while holding 1 bunch of flowers, 3 incense sticks, and 1 candle in their hands as a sign of respect for Buddha, Dharma and Sangha; they also offer food and other items to the monks in the sangha.

Visakha Puja Day

Visakha Puja day is also known as the Buddha Day and is celebrated on the first full moon day of May (except in a leap year when it is celebrated in the month of June).

This is considered a very special and holy day by Buddhists all over the world. On this day they celebrate the birth of Buddha, 2500 years ago, his enlightenment, and also remember his departure from this world.

Atthame Puja Day

Atthame Puja Day occurs on the 8th day of the waning moon of the 6th or 7th lunar month. This day occurs seven days after Visakha Puja Day and commemorates the day on which the body of Buddha was cremated. The ceremony is hosted at the temple and most of the participants are monks. The day is to remind Buddhists to behave and believe in good karma, to live their lives carefully, and to be aware that the body is impermanent: birth, old age, injury, and death are a part of life, and no one can escape them.

Asalha Puja Day

This day is also called Dharma Day and is celebrated on a full moon day sometime in July, the 8th lunar month. This day commemorates the first sermon of the Buddha to his first five disciples in the deer park at Sarnath, India.

Typically, on any special or holy day, Buddhists go to the temple, circumnavigate the chapel three times, take the five precepts, listen to discourses on Buddha's teachings and the life of Buddha, and participate in meditation and chanting along with fellow Buddhists.

Other Buddhist Holy Days

As I've just shown, there are 4 main holy days each year, but there are other, minor, Buddhist holy days (or *Thammasawana*) which occur four times a month with the following moon phases:

1. The 8th day of the waxing moon

2. The 15th day of the waxing moon (the full moon)

3. The 8th day of the waning moon

4. The 15th day of the waning moon or 14th day of waning moon in months with 30-days (the new moon).

On these days, Buddhists attend the ceremonies at the temple. Early in the morning, they prepare food, soft drink, desert, fruits, flowers, etc. and then take them to the temple. At the end of the ceremony, Buddhists pray for all the good things they have done and that they wish to go to their relatives who have passed away. In addition, they also wish that this good karma will radiate and go to all the people and animals that they have dealt with, and to ask for forgiveness for anything untoward they have done to them (intentionally or otherwise).

In the next section we will look at the Buddhist festivals.

Buddhist Festivals

The principal Buddhist festivals are Buddhist Lent Day (the start), the End of the Buddhist Lent Day, and Devorohana (or Tak-Bat-Devo).

Buddhist Lent Day

Buddhist Lent, or *Khao Phansa*, begins on the first waning day of the 8th lunar month, and lasts for three months to the 15th waxing day of the 11th lunar month. This period is during the rainy season and is when the monks temporarily stop the practice of travelling to other places to teach and give sermons; instead retreating to their monasteries.

This has been the practice since Buddha's time. Though their movement is itself restricted, no actual restriction is placed on their duty of spreading the Buddha's message. As such, people travel to the temples to listen to monks deliver sermons and to receive teachings within the confines of the monasteries.

This practice was started by Buddha as a way to address the concerns of the farmers who complained that wandering monks during the rainy season caused damage to their crops. As a result, Buddha imposed restrictions on the movement of the monks during the rainy season.

At this time, the young monks get a chance to train under the guidance of senior monks which can be an enriching experience for both parties.

This is also the period when the monks get ample time to meditate and to contemplate. This period is sort of a camping period as they have plenty of time to study the scriptures, to practice meditation, and can improve their morality, concentration and wisdom.

Furthermore, due to the presence and company of the senior monks, this is also a preferred and beneficial time for Buddhist believers to be ordained into the order. Additionally, and for that very same reason, large number of novices and families of the monks also congregate in the monasteries to benefit from the sermons and discourses delivered during that period. The novices get to pledge to follow the right path and to abstain from doing incorrect things such as smoking and consuming alcohol, and lots of positive energy is created from these gatherings.

End of the Buddhist Lent Day

The 15th day of the waxing moon of the 11th lunar month marks the end of Buddhist Lent (or *Auk Phansa*). This also marks the end of the rainy season and the monk's retreat period; this ending their restriction of movement. The End of Buddhist Lent Day is also one of the holy days for both monks and novices, and is the time the monks approach one another to atone for any mistake or offense caused or committed by them.

Buddhist believers (or novices) celebrate by gathering at the temples, offering food to the monks, praying, meditating, listening to Dharma and observing moral disciplines. It is a joyful day and in addition to the above, an alms giving ceremony known as Tak-Bat-Devo is organized on the following day to celebrate.

Devorohana (Tak-Bat-Devo)

Legend says that after Buddha attained enlightenment, he travelled extensively in India to deliver sermons and spread his message of Dharma. During these travels, he even enlightened and initiated his father, King Shoddodhana; his step-mother, Mahaprajapati; his wife, Yashodhara; his son, Rahula; and many others into the Buddhist tradition. It was then that he remembered his own mother, Queen Mahamaya, who passed away seven days after his birth. Lord Buddha wanted to repay her for her love and kindness so, seven years after attaining enlightenment, the Buddha went to the heaven where his mother was residing, stayed with her for three months, and taught her 'the profound truth' (*Abhidhamma Pitaka*). As the end of the three month retreat was approaching, the Buddha then came down from heaven and the people were overjoyed. They celebrated his coming back to the earth by offering food, practicing moral discipline and participating in the discourses and meditation.

This event came to be called Tak-Bat-Devo or Devorohana and, as mentioned, is usually celebrated the day after the last day of the Buddhist Lent.

Buddhist Ceremony

Offering Food to the Monks

Offering food is one of the oldest rituals of Buddhism and is considered a meritorious act because it teaches people not to be selfish, to share with others, and to promote generosity, kindness and compassion.

This ceremony has been practiced since the time of the Buddha, and monks and nuns leave their monastery very early in the morning carrying their alms bowl. They walk barefoot and silently in single file with the oldest or the senior most monk leading the group.

Those people willing to give alms stand in a line waiting for the monks to pass. Often, as a mark of respect, the laypeople kneel and some even remove their footwear as they place their offerings in the bowls. The ceremony takes place in a simple manner without even exchange of wishes and pleasantries. Sometimes, the senior monk in the group might wish to use this opportunity to deliver a brief sermon.

The practice of giving alms is not considered an act of charity but as an act aimed at developing a spiritual connection between householders and monks. While the householders take up the responsibility of providing for the basic, physical needs of the monks, the monks in turn look to fulfilling the higher, spiritual needs of the laypeople.

The offering of food to the monks can be done even in the temple or at home where people who are interested in offering food to the monks either bring food to the temple or invite the monks to their house.

When offering food to the monks in the Buddhist festival, *Tak-Bat-Devo*, the laypeople first sit in the temple for a sermon to be delivered. After the sermon the monks leave the main chapel where all the people would be waiting with their offerings. The monks, holding their bowls, walk in a straight line and people place their offerings in those bowls. When the bowl gets full, it is emptied into another plate by a layman so that the monk can continue taking alms. As always, women should take care not to touch the monks while placing food in the bowl.

After the monks have delivered a series of sermons and finished eating, all the food is placed on the table, and everybody there can partake of the food.

Become an Ordained Monk

The rules and procedures to be followed while carrying out an ordination ceremony are contained in the *Buddhist Monastic Rule* of the sangha.

The ceremony has not changed since the time of the Buddha and is carried out in Pali, the language of Buddhism at the time of origin, and which glorifies and establishes the importance of the ceremony. However, since Buddhism has permeated to various countries and cultures with different languages, the phrases in Pali are also translated into local languages for the convenience and understanding of family, friends, and well-wishers of the monks who have come to witness the ordaining ceremony.

To become a monk:

- One must be over 20 years of age and should have the consent of his parents.

- He should not have committed a crime such as murder, rape especially of a nun, causing injury to the Buddha, causing a rift in the sangha, pretend to be a monk without ordination, leaving the sangha to join another religion.

- Should not be a eunuch.

A person with an infectious disease, a fugitive, a debtor and one with physical disabilities cannot be ordained as they will be unable to stand the rigors of monastic life. But, if they have already been ordained, then their ordination will stand valid and cannot be dismissed on the above grounds.

For the ordination ceremony to take place, twelve monks from the sangha are required, one of whom should have been a monk for at least 10 years. This senior monk would later take charge as the preceptor of the would-be monk and take care of him during his monastic life while the young believer is expected to take care of the preceptor, just as he would take care of his father.

The ceremony begins with the parents of the young believer presenting him his monk robes and his bowl. At this stage, the young man is expected to ask his parents for forgiveness for any mistakes committed on his part in any form. With the parents' blessings, the would-be monk approaches the Sangha.

The person is then briefly instructed about the ceremony before being given his new name (this is to keep him reminded of his new life and the new purpose and responsibilities that come with it).

He is then sent to stand away from the main group of monks, following which two monks will go and test him on his suitability to be a monk. After examining him, the two monks return to the other monks and let them know about the test. The candidate is now called back and asked the same questions. They give their answers in front of all the monks.

Since one cannot be forced into monkhood, the young man is supposed to make a formal request to the Sangha to be ordained as a monk. All monks participating in the ordination should sit within arm's length of each other, and the two monks of the sangha make an announcement that the person has made a formal request for ordination and that he has been found suitable to be made a monk. They continue to propose this two more times. This is the time when any objection (if any) to the ordination of the person can be raised and any objection leads to the denial of monkhood for the person. In the event of no objection, the person is declared a monk.

The preceptor of the newly ordained monk will then instruct him on the four disrobing offences which are to be treated as the four dangers to monkhood and which are to be avoided: sexual intercourse, murder, false claims of attainment, and stealing. He will also receive instructions on the four basic needs of a monk: food gathered as alms, robes made of rags, a shelter under a tree, and medicines made from urine. With these instructions the ceremony comes to a close.

Chapter 4. Mind and Wisdom Exercises

Wise Reflection

Wise reflection or *Yoniso Manasikara* means using the mind skilfully.

Using the mind skilfully is to understand and gain an insight into what the consequences of our thoughts and actions would be like, to understand the true nature of things, and to accept the hard truths of life.

The literal meaning of Yoniso is 'the place of origin from where everything starts and from where everything begins', but the true meaning says that Yoniso means 'to get to the core of something in order to perfect your understanding with regard to the consequences'. Manasikara means to direct, or lead, the attention to the core (heart, depth).

It must be understood that plain concentration is not enough to gain wisdom. To gain wisdom requires the ability to pay wise attention to accomplish things. Buddha was deeply interested in the subject of wise reflection and said the following about it

"I say that the getting rid of anxieties and troubles is possible for one who knows and sees, not for one who does not know and see."

According to Buddha, a person who knows and sees is the one who reflects wisely, and the person who does not know and see is the one who reflects unwisely.

For example, a person who reflects unwisely will start to see anxieties and troubles that have not yet arisen; whereas, a person who reflects unwisely and who is already facing anxieties and troubles will see their effects increase. In contrast, a person who reflects wisely will either never see these troubles or anxieties, or will be able to avoid them when they do appear—wise reflection can, and will, make them disappear.

From his enlightenment until his death, the Buddha kept emphasizing that mental suffering is caused by wrong thinking; and this is where Yoniso Manasikara comes to the rescue: wise reflection helps one to develop and nurture the wisdom and intelligence to consider things using critical and analytical reflection, as well as systematic and reasoned attention with a view to developing right thinking.

Insight Meditation

Insight meditation, or Vipassana, is the process of knowing and gaining proper understanding about oneself.

When we experience suffering, we usually blame our external world; this could be God, it could be people, or it could be circumstances. However, Buddha identified this is incorrect. In reality, our suffering is actually caused by our own internal, not external, world: it is our own thoughts, feelings, and emotions that cause pain and suffering to us.

Consequently, changing our external world or trying to manipulate our external world is no guarantee of happiness. What can give us everlasting happiness is a mind which is pure and free of unhealthy thoughts, and one that is free from desire and ignorance (the root causes of suffering). This purification is possible with Vipassana meditation.

Vipassana is a technique that ensures success only if we are willing to devote our efforts to our internal world, instead of placing all this responsibility on our external world.

Meditation techniques can be classified into two types: insight meditation (Vipassana), and tranquillity meditation (concentration).

In tranquillity meditation (concentration), we practice by trying to focus our mind on one object until we develop enough concentration, attain stillness, calmness, and are able to filter out all mental afflictions, such as anger, stress, jealousy, hatred, impatience, etc. The only problem here is that when one stops meditating, the mental afflictions can come straight back and reside where they were before—in our minds. Insight meditation, or Vipassana is different.

Vipassana does not stop at developing plain concentration, it also develops wisdom. Vipassana is about developing mindfulness. You see, in mindfulness, we do not fix out attention on one thing, we just let things, ideas, thoughts, emotions, feelings, etc., come and pass but without our reacting to them. Vipassana is about realizing and making note of each feeling, sensation, and emotion but without responding to it. Eventually, these unhealthy mental factors vacate our minds leaving it pure.

Vipassana deals with dissecting the mind to separate reality from delusion, and is a powerful and intense form of dissecting the mind to examine its components. It's almost confronting the truth and reality with a view to gaining freedom from suffering and, ultimately, enlightenment.

Conclusion

In conclusion, I hope you've enjoyed reading my book. I also hope that now you've looked at the principle aspects of Buddhism, I am confident that by understanding the topics that we've covered, you will see how this may perhaps assist you in looking at, evaluating, and improving your own particular situation (if you do indeed need to do so).

Regardless of whether you are actually a Buddhist yourself, I hope you can see that by making small changes to your daily routine, and perhaps by adopting some of these practices yourself, it can not only help to improve your life, but can help in other areas to: your outlook, your relationships with others, with how you view your surroundings, and with those whom you come into contact with.

Please Leave a Review on Amazon

Finally, if you have enjoyed the book, I would be most grateful if you would leave a review on Amazon: without reviews, authors like me really struggle. So you would not only be helping others, but me too.

Make Meditation a Part of Your Life

Meditation is a wonderful practice that you should try and build into your schedule as it brings enormous benefits (that most successful people in business and in life have made meditation an integral part of their routines should speak volumes to you); and, I would highly recommend my book, *A Beginner's Guide to Meditation* to also help you on **your path to a meaningful life**.

Author's Page

Duangta Wanthong Mondi is Thai and a Buddhist. She lives and works in the North-east of Thailand as an English teacher in a Thai State school.

Duangta has an M. Ed. In Teaching English as a Foreign Language (TEFL), and has co-authored a series of books to help English speakers learn Thai.

The series is called *Quest (**Qu**ick, **E**asy, **S**imple **T**hai)* and consists of:

- *Learning Thai, Your Great Adventure*

- *Learn Thai Alphabet with Memory Aids to Your Great Adventure*

- *The Perfect Thai Phrasebook*

- *How to Read Thai*

- *The Learn Thai Alphabet application* (web and iPad app)

- *The Learn Thai Numbers application* (web and iPad app)

Website – *http://www.teachermondi.com*

Facebook - *https://www.facebook.com/teachermondi*

Bibliography

Buddhist Beliefs. (n.d.). Retrieved June 27, 2015, from Religion
 Facts: http://www.religionfacts.com/buddhism/beliefs

Hagen, S. (2013). *Buddhism Plain and Simple*. Singapore: Tuttle.

Hanh, T. N. (1999). *The Heart of the Buddha's Teaching:
 Transforming Suffering into Peace, Joy, and Liberation*.
 New York: Broadway Books.

History of Buddhism. (n.d.). Retrieved June 26, 2015, from About
 Buddhism: http://www.aboutbuddhism.org/history-of-
 buddhism.htm/

Lama, D. (2006). *The Universe in a Single Atom: The Convergence
 of Science and Spirituality*. New York: Harmony.

Lama, D. (2013). *What Matters Most: Conversations on Anger,
 Compassion, and Action*. Charlottesville: Hampton Roads
 Publishing.

Sayagaw, M. (2009, March 16). *What is Threefold Training* .
 Retrieved June 28, 2015, from Yellow Robe:
 http://www.yellowrobe.com/practice/the-threefold-
 training/221-what-is-threefold-training.html

Thuan, X. (N.D.). *Science and Buddhism*. Retrieved June 25, 2015,
 from Universitie Interdisciplinaire De Paris:
 http://uip.edu/en/articles-en/science-and-buddhism

Verhoeven, M. (2013, Summer). Science through Buddhist Eyes.
 The New Atlantis, 39, 107-118. Retrieved from The new
 Atlantis.

Printed in Great Britain
by Amazon